Table of Contents

Hawkeye's Adventures	1
Michael Jordan	3
Crazy Horse	5
Korczak Ziolkowski	7
Buried Alive	9
Wayne Gretzky	11
Edgar Allen Poe	12
Pandora's Box	13
Curse of the Jade Tulip	14
The Clydesdales	15
The Trojan Horse	16
Space Camp	17
The New Wheel	18
Margaret Bourke-White	19
St. Elmo's Fire	20
Moby Dick	21
Ian Fleming	22
Sports Medicine	24
Lorraine Hansberry	26
The Sherpa	28
The Mountain Lion	30
Toying with New Ideas	32
The Birth of an Island	33
The Spectre Bridegroom	34
Treetop Balloons	35
Dogs That Make a Difference	36
The Rescuers	37
Rudyard Kipling	38
The Sacred Ganges	39
Captain Courageous	40
The Cobra	42
The Smallest Warrior	44

© Milliken Publishing Company

Teaching Guide

Introduction

This book is one of six in a series designed to encourage the reading enjoyment of young students. Subject matter was carefully chosen to correspond to student interests. Skills were selected to reinforce understanding of the readings and to promote confidence in independent reading.

Content

The contents of each book have been drawn from seven specific categories: 1) biography, 2) amazing facts, 3) mystery and intrigue, 4) sports stars and events, 5) visual and performing arts, 6) wonders in science and nature, and 7) excerpts from mythology and literature.

The popular biographies, sports figures, and artists give students an opportunity to identify with people who are familiar to them. Those figures who are unknown to the students' experience give them clues to the wide diversity of current society in many countries. A look behind the scenes of a famous life holds a never-ending fascination.

In addition to spy stories and tales of ghostly encounters, the mystery selections often offer a puzzling situation to solve or the beginning of a story which must be completed by the reader.

Science and nature selections are chosen to generate interest in new and untapped areas of the readers' knowledge and to encourage them to explore further.

Samples of a wide variety of stories from mythology and literature have been included. It is hoped that this brief encounter with some of the great story lines will motivate the student to seek out and read the entire selection.

Skills

The skills employed in this series are drawn from traditional educational objectives. The five comprehension areas practiced in this series are: main idea, recognition of significant details, use of context clues for determining word meaning, inference, and drawing conclusions. All categories are not necessarily represented at the conclusion of each story. Questioning format varies from book to book to avoid predictability. Where space permits, a follow-through activity has been included. These are expected to lead to self-motivated reading or to valuable discussion. The activity also gives the teacher an opportunity to award extra credit.

Upon completion of each collection of stories and accompanying skill activities, students should show improvement in the areas practiced; i.e., the ability to locate, evaluate, and predict, as well as to conduct study and research.

Readability

The reading level of each book is essentially two years below the interest level. Readability levels were confirmed by the Spache formula for the lower grades and the Dale-Chall formula for the upper grades. Each book is suitable for a variety of students working at a range of reading levels. The lower readability allows older students with reading deficiencies to enjoy high-interest content with minimum frustration. The comprehension activities provide a growth opportunity for capable students as well. The high-interest content should help to motivate students at any level.

The teacher should keep in mind that supplying easy-to-read content provides a good setting for learning new skills. Thus, comprehension development can best take place where vocabulary and sentence constraints ensure student understanding. It should be obvious that the concept of main idea, as well as the nature of an inference, can be seen best where the total content of a selection is well within a reader's grasp.

Finally, the material is dedicated to the principle that the more a student reads, the better he or she reads, and the greater is the appreciation of the printed word.

© Milliken Publishing Company

Answer Key

Page 2
1. c
2. a
3. b
4. a
5. c
6. b
7. a
8. b

Page 4
1. c
2. 28
3. a
4. a

Page 6
1. c
2. b
3. b
4. a
5. a
6. c
7. c
8. c
9. c
10. b

Page 8
1. b
2. a
3. b
4. c
5. c

Page 10
1. b
2. a
3. c
4. c
5. c
6. b
7. a
8. c
9. c

Page 11
1. b
2. c
3. b
4. a
5. a
6. c

Page 12
1. c
2. a
3. b
4. a
5. c

Page 13
1. b
2. a
3. a

Page 15
1. b
2. c
3. a
4. c
5. b

Page 16
1. a
2. c
3. a
4. b
5. b

Page 17
1. c
2. a
3. c
4. b
5. a

Page 19
1. a
2. c
3. b
4. c
5. b

Page 20
1. b
2. c
3. a
4. a
5. b

Page 21
1. b
2. a
3. a
4. b
5. b

Page 23
1. a
2. b
3. c
4. b
5. c

Page 25
1. c
2. b
3. a
4. c
5. b
6. a

Page 27
1. c
2. b
3. b
4. a
5. c

Page 29
1. b
2. c
3. b
4. a
5. a
6. b

Page 31
1. b
2. a
3. c
4. c
5. a

Page 32
1. c
2. b
3. a
4. c

Page 33
1. c
2. a
3. b
4. c
5. b
6. a
7. a

Page 34
1. c
2. b
3. a

Page 35
1. b
2. a
3. b
4. b
5. c

Page 36
1. c
2. a
3. b
4. a
5. b

Page 37
1. a
2. c
3. b
4. c
5. b

Page 38
1. c
2. c
3. b
4. a
5. c

Page 39
1. b
2. c
3. a
4. c
5. b
6. c

Page 41
1. b
2. c
3. a
4. a
5. b
6. a
7. b
8. c
9. c

Page 43
1. c
2. b
3. a
4. a
5. c
6. b
7. a
8. a

Page 44
1. b
2. a
3. b
4. c
5. c
6. b

Hawkeye's Adventures
(Adapted from *The Last of the Mohicans* by James Fenimore Cooper)

Hawkeye, a frontiersman, lived in America during the 1700s. He was born on the frontier and lived alone in the woods. At an early age, he learned how to use a rifle. Over the years, he became known as an excellent shot. His skill with the rifle saved his life more than once.

Hawkeye lived through a dangerous time in America. In 1757, the country was mostly wilderness, and many forces were fighting to control it. The French and English were battling with each other and with the Native Americans for rule of the land. Many Native American tribes were fighting among themselves as well.

Since he lived during such an active time, Hawkeye had many adventures. One adventure ended in a sad way for Hawkeye. He was tracking in the woods with his lifelong friend, Chingachgook. Chingachgook was a member of the Mohican tribe. His son, Uncas, had just joined the two men when they were surprised by a group of travelers. Two young English ladies, Alice and Cora Munro, were trying to make their way through the wilderness to Fort William Henry. Their father, Colonel Munro, commanded the fort, which was now under attack by the French. The girls wanted to be with their father. They were accompanied by two men from the English Army. The whole group was being led by Magua, an evil Huron Indian.

Hawkeye spotted Magua at once. He knew that this treacherous man was probably kidnapping the group instead of guiding them to the fort. Magua, suspecting that he had been seen, left the group and went into the woods. Hawkeye and the Mohicans took the group to hide in the safety of some caves. In the morning, they were attacked by Magua and his band of Hurons. Hawkeye, Chingachgook, and Uncas fought bravely and successfully. Magua escaped into the woods.

The group started toward the fort. They had to slip past French troops to get there. With Hawkeye as guide, the girls finally reached their father at Fort William Henry. The Colonel was very happy to see his daughters, but the happiness did not last long. Magua and another tribe attacked the fort and kidnapped the girls.

Uncas was very upset by this. He and Cora had fallen in love, and Uncas did not want anything to happen to her. He started after them, but in a short time, he, too, was captured by the Hurons. Hawkeye and

continued . . .

Chingachgook hid in the woods and waited for the right opportunity. Then, disguised in beaver coats and animal heads, the two helped Uncas escape and attacked the Hurons. In the bitter battle, all the enemies, including Magua, were killed. Unfortunately, Uncas and Cora died during the fighting too.

Hawkeye helped Chingachgook bury his son and Cora. Chingachgook was very sad. Uncas was his only son as well as the last brave of the Mohican tribe. Chingachgook felt very alone. Hawkeye was able to cheer him a little. He promised to remain with his best friend, Chingachgook, forever. The two men set off through the woods in search of new adventures.

Main Idea
1. Hawkeye spent his life
   a. killing Native Americans.
   b. helping the English army.
   c. surviving in the wilderness.

Significant Details
2. Uncas belonged to the
   a. Mohican tribe.
   b. Huron tribe.
   c. Magua tribe.
3. Hawkeye was well known for his
   a. friendship with Native Americans.
   b. skill with a rifle.
   c. wood carvings.
4. Alice and Cora wanted to visit their father at
   a. Fort William Henry.
   b. English Army Fort.
   c. Fort Colonel Munro.

Context Clues
5. Magua was a *treacherous* man.
   a. brave
   b. loyal
   c. dangerous

6. Hawkeye and Chingachgook *disguised* themselves.
   a. planned a bitter attack
   b. changed their appearance
   c. gave themselves up

Inference
7. Hawkeye was a good person because
   a. he risked his life to help others.
   b. he lived alone in the woods.
   c. he knew how to use a rifle.

Drawing Conclusions
8. America must not have had its own government at the time this story took place because
   a. the country was still nothing but woods.
   b. other countries were still fighting for its control.
   c. the French were in control of the land.

Following Through
9. Read James F. Cooper's original *The Last of the Mohicans*. Try reading other stories from his *Leather-Stocking Tales*. Find out what names Hawkeye is known by in these other tales.

Michael Jordan

Every sport has its own unique words or sayings. One of basketball's most descriptive phrases is "hang time." This is the length of time a player can stay off the floor and up in the air. The longer he can "hang" in the air close to the basket, the more points he is likely to score.

Basketball fans agree that Michael Jordan, the superstar of the NBA, has the longest hang time on the court. He also has one of the longest lists of awards. He was named College Player of the Year and Rookie of the Year and later became a two-time Olympic Gold Medalist for the U.S., top scorer for seven seasons, and the Most Valuable Player three different times.

Michael played guard for the Chicago Bulls. His average score per game was at least 28 points. The average attendance at his games doubled. Fans couldn't wait to see Michael glide and hang. Even when the Bulls were on the road, attendance in other cities increased when Michael was in town. Michael soon became an idol for teenagers and a star for adults.

Basketball was not always easy for Michael. He was so slow and weak in high school that he barely made the team. He continued developing his skills and played at the University of North Carolina during college. Soon he became known for his fast feet and overall speed.

Michael's personality seems to match his skills. He always seems happy and friendly. His patience with reporters and children is endless. Everyone admires the man who led the Bulls in scoring, rebounding, assists, free-throw percentages, and steals. Even though Michael has retired from the basketball courts, fans still appreciate him as he makes appearances at children's hospitals, hosts fundraisers for charity, or just shakes hands with the fans in the street. Michael promises to keep up with his television appearances and moviegoers hope that Michael may star in another motion picture. Whether or not Michael will be seen again on the big screen, Jordan will always be remembered as one of basketball's greatest players.

Main Idea
1. Michael Jordan is mainly known for his
   a. assists and rebounds.
   b. high school career.
   c. hang time on the court.

Significant Details
2. How many points did Michael average each game? _____

Inference
3. It is easy to tell Michael was popular with the fans because
   a. attendance at his games doubled.
   b. he can "hang" in the air.
   c. he is pleasant to reporters.

Drawing Conclusions
4. Why do you think fans call Michael Jordan a superstar?
   a. He has an impressive list of accomplishments on the court.
   b. He signs every autograph and often poses for pictures.
   c. He is seen in many television commercials.

Following Through
5. Michael took a short break from basketball and tried his hand at another sport. Find out what sport it was, how successful he was, and if this sport might be a part of Michael's future.

Crazy Horse

Before white settlers came to the Black Hills of South Dakota, this area was a sacred place to the Sioux Indians. They called these hills *Paha Sapa*. The Sioux tribes held special ceremonies in the hills. They believed that Paha Sapa was a place for the spirits of dead warriors. It was thought that when a great warrior died, his spirit would go to Paha Sapa to get used to the great beauty of the land. Then the spirit would move on to the supreme beauty of a place called Great Paradise.

Crazy Horse was a great chief of the Sioux Indians. He and his tribe fought to stop the United States government from taking Indian land. In 1867, the U.S. government said that the Sioux could keep the area of land that included the Black Hills. In 1874, however, the U.S. government broke its promise and allowed white settlers to come into the Black Hills to search for gold. The Sioux fought many battles to keep the land.

Finally, they ran short of food and realized that there were many more U.S. troops than Sioux warriors. The Sioux gave up their fight. Crazy Horse was killed by a soldier while jailed in an army fort.

Years later, a group of Sioux called the Crazy Horse Foundation secured a piece of the Black Hills area from the U.S. government. The part they chose is Thunderhead Mountain. Chief Henry Standing Bear asked a sculptor named Korczak Ziolkowski to carve a special work on Thunderhead Mountain to honor Crazy Horse.

Ziolkowski was proud to do the work. He started on the carving immediately. Plans called for the statue to be 563 feet high and 641 feet long. This was quite a big task. Ziolkowski spent the rest of his life carving this Indian statue. Unfortunately, he died in 1982 before the statue was finished.

continued...

At the base of Thunderhead Mountain, the Foundation built a museum for Indian artifacts. Outside the museum is a small model of the Crazy Horse statue. This statue shows Crazy Horse seated on his horse. He is pointing the way to where the monument will stand. With money raised at the museum, Ziolkowski's wife and ten children are continuing work on the statue. Parts of the Indian's head and arm, and the curve of the horse's head can be seen emerging from the mountain. When it is finished, the Crazy Horse Memorial will be the largest carving in the world.

Main Idea
1. The memorial on Thunderhead Mountain will honor
   a. the Black Hills.
   b. Korczak Ziolkowski.
   c. Chief Crazy Horse.

Significant Details
2. Thunderhead Mountain is located
   a. in North Dakota.
   b. in the Black Hills.
   c. in South Carolina.
3. The Crazy Horse Memorial is now helped by
   a. the United States government.
   b. a Foundation.
   c. the president.
4. Who asked the sculptor to carve the statue of Crazy Horse?
   a. Chief Henry Standing Bear
   b. Ziolkowski's wife
   c. the governor of South Dakota

Context Clues
5. Parts of the statue are *emerging* from the mountain.
   a. coming into view
   b. sinking into the ground
   c. covered with rock dust
6. In the story, *honor* means
   a. to buy.
   b. to find.
   c. show respect.
7. The museum at the base of Thunderhead Mountain is filled with Indian *artifacts*.
   a. book written about Indians
   b. paintings that show Indians
   c. objects made by Indians of years gone by

Inference
8. How do you know that the Black Hills area is a beautiful sight?
   a. Everyone wants to build monuments there.
   b. It is full of large trees.
   c. Indian legend compares its beauty to Paradise.
9. *Paha Sapa* means
   a. Thunderhead Mountain.
   b. Crazy Horse.
   c. Black Hills.

Drawing Conclusions
10. Ziolkowski must have instilled his respect for the Sioux in his own family because they
    a. donated money to the statue.
    b. continue to work on the statue.
    c. write books about Indian ways of life.

Korczak Ziolkowski

Korczak Ziolkowski was born with determination. His parents died when he was just a small baby, and he grew up in a series of foster homes. He had to work hard to please those raising him, and he worked hard to please himself. By the time he was 16, Korczak was ready to make his own way in the world. He wanted to learn a useful skill by attending a technical school, but he didn't have the money for tuition. Determined, Korczak got a tough job on Boston's waterfront and earned enough money to go to school at the same time.

At 18, Korczak began experimenting with woodcarving and furniture making. He made beautifully ornate pieces and sold this furniture for extra money. Although Korczak had found a talent that was very profitable, he still wasn't satisfied. Korczak was interested in sculpture. He loved the look of smooth statues and polished marble.

Korczak had absolutely no idea how to begin with sculpture. He had never had art lessons or formal training. Determined to sculpt, Korczak began studying on his own. He scrutinized the famous statues and works of art around town. He noticed the flow of the statues and the cut of the stone. Eventually, with some crude tools, Korczak began working on his own sculpture.

Within a short period of time, Korczak knew he had found his true calling. People began commissioning sculptures from Ziolkowski. Many wanted to own a piece of his art work. One of his marble statues won first prize at the New York's World Fair. Korczak opened his own sculpture studio and started a very successful career.

All of Ziolkowski's hard work and determination paid off when he was asked to work on the carving of Mt. Rushmore. Korczak served as the assistant to the famous lead sculptor, Gutzon Borglum. He learned a lot on that project, and it was the knowledge he acquired from Borglum that helped him begin what would be his most important project of all.

Ziolkowski served two years in World War II. After the war, people all over Europe asked him to stay and do their sculptures. He could have had a very lucrative career in Europe, but Korczak had other plans. He had heard about the history of the Sioux Indian tribes in America, and how the U.S. government, in 1867, had broken its promise and had taken the Sioux land. Perhaps to make up for his government's wrongdoing, Korczak decided to devote the rest of his life to honoring the Sioux people. He was asked to carve a special mountain statue as a tribute to the brave Sioux leader, Chief Crazy Horse.

Korczak proudly moved to the Black Hills of South Dakota where he and his wife, Ruth, began the lifelong task of carving the mountain. Korczak and Ruth had ten children, and together they raised them with a sense of humor and a respect for the Sioux people. Because there were so many Ziolkowski children running around the carving site, Korczak had a one-room schoolhouse set up at the base of the mountain. A certified teacher was hired and the schoolhouse was filled—with mostly Ziolkowski's children! There the children learned first-hand about the history of their nation, as well as the techniques and skill in carving a huge mountain.

Korczak Ziolkowski died in 1982, but his work did not. Korczak had asked Ruth and their children to carry on the work. "Go slowly," he told them. "You must do it right."

continued . . .

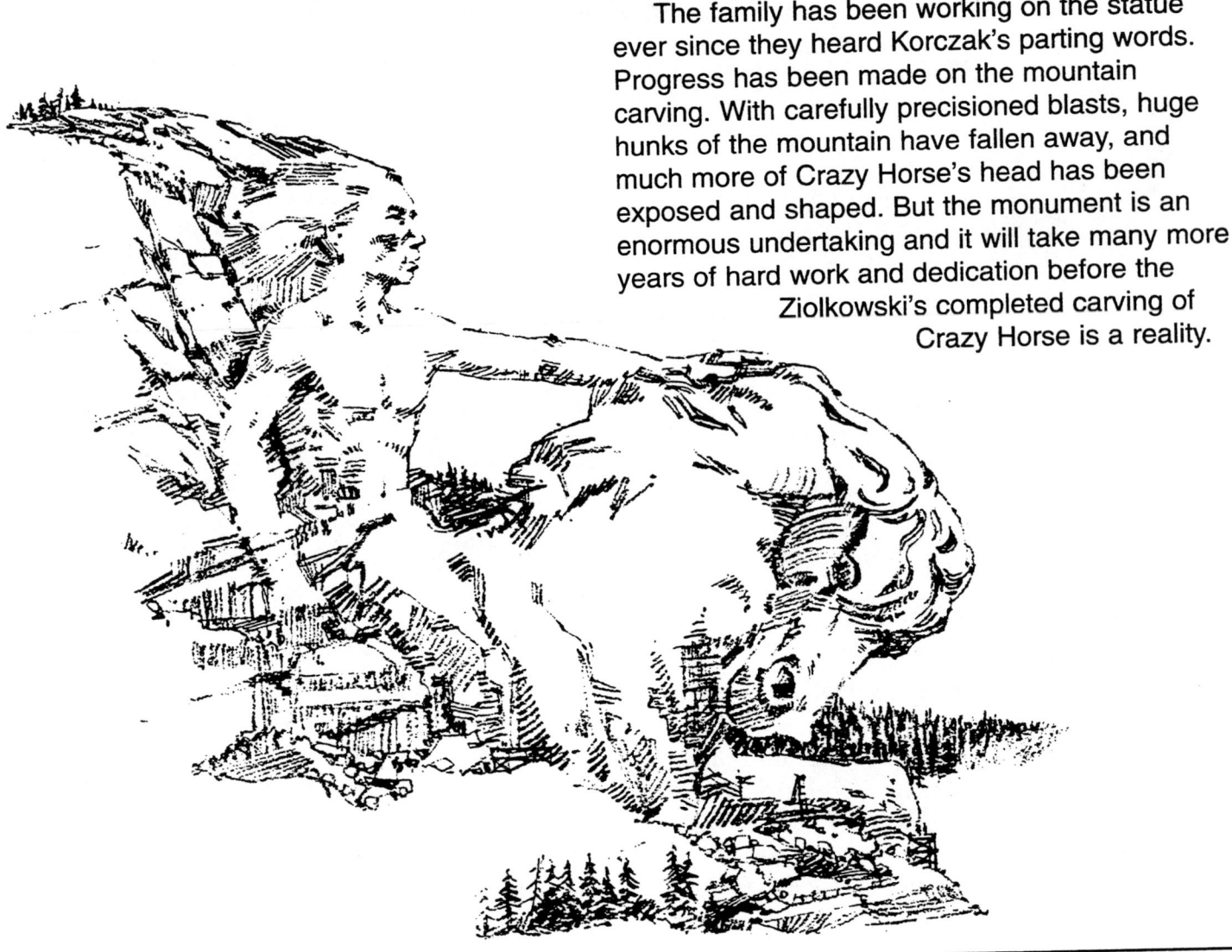

The family has been working on the statue ever since they heard Korczak's parting words. Progress has been made on the mountain carving. With carefully precisioned blasts, huge hunks of the mountain have fallen away, and much more of Crazy Horse's head has been exposed and shaped. But the monument is an enormous undertaking and it will take many more years of hard work and dedication before the Ziolkowski's completed carving of Crazy Horse is a reality.

Main Idea
1. Korczak Ziolkowski's life ambition was to
   a. become a great sculptor.
   b. honor a great culture.
   c. carve Mt. Rushmore.

Significant Details
2. Korczak learned much of his trade
   a. on his own.
   b. working on Boston's waterfront.
   c. by taking art lessons.
3. Korczak won a prize for his
   a. ornate furniture.
   b. marble sculpture.
   c. woodworking.

Inference
4. Why was Ziolkowski called a man of determination?
   a. He was determined to be wealthy and successful.
   b. He persevered when people told him his art was not acceptable.
   c. He persevered without formal training and assistance.

Context Clues
5. Korczak gave up a *lucrative* career.
   a. European career
   b. an easy career
   c. a profitable career

Drawing Conclusions
6. Do you think the Ziolkowski children will finish their father's work? Why or why not?

_____
_____
_____

Buried Alive

(Adapted from *Fall of the House of Usher* by Edgar Allan Poe)

Allen had been traveling by horseback all day. At nightfall, he finally reached the gloomy mansion, the House of Usher. This was the home of Allen's boyhood friend, Roderick Usher. Roderick was very ill, and Allen had come to visit him. As he followed the butler through the damp, musty hall and up the creaking stairs, Allen began to think that the gloominess of the house had something to do with his friend's illness. He was sure of it when he came to Roderick's room which had dark drapes and was dimly lit. Roderick, who was lying on a couch, pulled himself up and welcomed his friend.

Allen could see that Roderick was indeed very ill. He began to think of ways to cheer Roderick. In the next few days, the two friends talked and read together. Gradually Allen realized that Roderick was worried. His twin sister, Madeline had a strange sickness. She seemed to be wasting away, and doctors could do nothing for her.

Later that week, Roderick came to Allen with the sad news of Madeline's death. Roderick did not want to bury her in the family graveyard. He asked Allen to help him keep his sister closer.

The two men carried Madeline's coffin down into the depths of the mansion. They placed the coffin on a stand in a basement room. As Allen looked at Madeline, she seemed peaceful. He noticed that her lips were turned up in a slight smile. Allen helped Roderick tightly screw down the wooden coffin lid and bolt the huge iron door at the entrance to the room. Allen decided to stay and comfort his friend a while longer.

About a week after Madeline's burial, a terrible storm woke Allen. The wind, thunder, and lightning were fierce. Suddenly, Roderick stumbled into Allen's room and fell onto a chair. He was white and trembling. From somewhere below them, there came a sound of wood being splintered. This was followed by a thin scream. Next came a scraping noise like that of the opening of a heavy door. Now Allen, too, was shaking with fright. Suddenly, the bedroom door blew open. In the hall stood Madeline. Her dress was covered with blood. She was shaking and crying as she held out her arms toward her brother.

"She was not dead!" said Roderick. "It was only a trance. I buried my sister alive!"

continued . . .

Roderick rushed to his sister. Madeline fell forward into his arms, and the two of them sank to the floor. By the time Allen reached them, both Roderick and Madeline were dead.

That was enough. Allen fled from this house of horrors. As he rushed across a bridge and away from the mansion, a vivid bolt of lightning flashed. Allen looked back. The entire mansion had split apart, and he watched as it slowly sank into the murky water that surrounded it. Such was the fall of the House of Usher.

Main Idea
1. This story is mainly about
    a. a thunderstorm.
    b. events in a gloomy mansion.
    c. Madeline Usher.

Significant Details
2. Allen came to the House of Usher because
    a. his friend Roderick was ill.
    b. Roderick had a beautiful sister.
    c. he liked old mansions.
3. Roderick's main worry was
    a. fixing up the House of Usher.
    b. helping Allen.
    c. the strange illness of his sister.
4. As Allen looked at Madeline in the coffin, he noticed that
    a. she was not dead.
    b. she looked just like Roderick.
    c. her lips curved in a smile.
5. Roderick did not want to bury Madeline in the graveyard because
    a. she had asked him not to.
    b. she was not dead.
    c. he wanted her to be near him.

Context Clues
6. A *vivid* flash of lightning would be
    a. dangerous.
    b. extremely bright.
    c. noisy.
7. A *trance* is something like a
    a. deep sleep.
    b. wooden coffin.
    c. graveyard.

Inference
8. The sound like splintering wood heard by Roderick and Allen was
    a. just their imagination.
    b. only the wind and rain.
    c. Madeline trying to open the coffin.

Drawing Conclusions
9. Why did Allen run away from the House of Usher?
    a. He knew it was going to fall.
    b. He was very ill.
    c. All the strange events frightened him.

Following Through
10. Read more stories and poems by Edgar Allan Poe. Then try writing a horror story of your own. Share it with the class.

Wayne Gretzky, King of the Ice

Wayne Gretzky was voted the National Hockey League's Most Valuable Player of the Year seven times. Many hockey fans find Wayne's outstanding record even more unusual because of his slight build. Compared to his teammates, he is relatively small (under 6 feet) and lightweight (170 lbs.). Wayne is neither a tricky skater nor a hard shooter, yet his record for assisting and scoring goals has amazed fans of every team. How does he do it?

Wayne's training started in his own backyard. Wayne's father was a minor league hockey player, but he never pushed Wayne toward hockey. He did flood the family's backyard in freezing weather, though. This made a skating rink for young Wayne. Wayne's father even put up some lights so Wayne could practice at night. This was Wayne's training place. Wayne whizzed around cans, jumped over sticks, and shot goal after goal. By the time he was 17, he was playing hockey with the Edmonton Oilers of Canada.

With the Oilers, Wayne found great teammates and great hometown fans. He began a long career of breaking just about every record in hockey. From his skating and leaping on the backyard ice rink, Wayne developed an unusual skill. He could stay clear of head-on crashes with other players. This saved him a lot of time and penalties during games.

Wayne could slide sideways very well. He could also stop and turn very quickly. It was hard to match his skill. His list of records is also hard to match. Although retired now, Wayne is still paid an important tribute. In spite of years of hockey battles, Wayne is still known as the "Gentleman on Ice."

Main Idea
1. The main person in this story is a
   a. coach of the Edmonton Oilers.
   b. hockey star.
   c. roller skater.

Significant Details
2. What did Wayne's father set up in his backyard?
   a. a hockey arena
   b. a set of weights
   c. a homemade ice rink
3. How many years did Wayne win the Most Valuable Player award?
   a. ten
   b. seven
   c. seventeen
4. How has Wayne avoided penalties during games?
   a. by avoiding head-on crashes
   b. by jumping over sticks
   c. by amazing fans

Context Clues
5. A *tribute* is something like
   a. praise.
   b. winning.
   c. losing.

Drawing Conclusions
6. Which do you think is true of Wayne?
   a. He is very boastful.
   b. He is very tall and strong.
   c. He is very well-liked by fans.

Edgar Allan Poe

Edgar Allan Poe was born in Boston in 1809. His parents were both actors and probably expected Edgar to join them on the stage. But the course of Edgar's life changed when his father left the family and his mother died before Edgar reached the age of three.

Young Edgar was taken in by a businessman from Virginia, John Allan, and his wife. The Allans raised Edgar and sent him to private schools. When he was old enough, they enrolled him in college at the University of Virginia. Instead of studying at college, Edgar began drinking and gambling. John Allan was disappointed in Edgar and refused to pay his debts. Edgar was forced to drop out of school.

Edgar left Virginia and the Allan family and moved back to his hometown, Boston. There he published his first piece of writing, *Tamerlane and Other Poems*, in 1827. It was then that Poe knew he had a talent for writing.

Edgar soon married, but his young wife became very ill. In order to pay for his wife's doctor bills, Edgar took several jobs as an editor of newspapers and magazines, but continued to write. He published several volumes of poetry and earned recognition as a skilled poet. His descriptive images and perfect meter made his poems outstanding pieces of writing that are still read today.

Although Poe loved poetry, he realized that publishing short stories would earn him more money. Poe became the first writer to publish detective stories. "The Gold Bug" was a story about searching for buried treasure. Poe's mystery and horror stories were very popular, too. "The Fall of the House of Usher," "The Tell-Tale Heart," and "Pit and the Pendulum" both frightened and excited readers. "The Murders in the Rue Morgue" and "The Mystery of Marie Roget" are examples of Poe's well-developed plots with unusual twists that keep the reader in suspense until the end of the story.

Poe's work is still enjoyed today. Even though Edgar Allan Poe's life seemed to be filled with sadness, his writing reflects some of the more human aspects of life. He was able to go deep into his characters' minds and make them realistic for the reader. Perhaps it is this realistic quality mixed with excitement that gives Poe's stories their longevity and lasting interest.

Main Idea
1. Edgar Allan Poe is known for his
   a. work as an editor.
   b. life as an actor.
   c. stories and poems.

Significant Details
2. Poe preferred to write
   a. poetry.
   b. mysteries.
   c. short stories.

Context Clues
3. Poe's stories have *longevity*.
   a. They are very long.
   b. Their appeal lasts a long time.
   c. They are written about tall people.

Inferences
4. Poe's unusual childhood probably
   a. influenced his writing.
   b. made him refuse to marry.
   c. kept him from becoming famous.

Drawing Conclusions
5. If Poe became an actor, he probably would have starred in
   a. comedies.
   b. Broadway musicals.
   c. murder mysteries.

Pandora's Box
(Adapted from Greek mythology)

In Greek mythology, the beautiful Pandora was the first woman on earth. Zeus, the head of the gods, ordered his son Hephaetus to create her. Hephaetus was the god of crafts. He had built palaces for each of the gods. He had also made Zeus' famous thunderbolts and wonderful armor for the warrior Achilles. Creating a woman was a big task. Hephaetus molded earth and water into a lovely woman to send to earth.

This woman was named Pandora, meaning "all-gifts." She was given this name because the gods and goddesses gave her many gifts. One gave her beauty. Another gave her knowledge. Still others gave her beautiful clothes. Zeus gave her the most interesting gift of all. It was a small, black box. The box was tightly locked. The other gods warned Pandora never to open Zeus' box.

Many men on earth fell in love with Pandora, but she chose to marry one named Epimetheus. Pandora began to enjoy life and forgot all about the black box. Then one day, when her husband was away, Pandora was feeling bored. She came across the box. It was half hidden in the corner of a room. She looked at it carefully. There did not seem to be anything special about it. She wondered why the gods had told her not to open it.

Finally, Pandora decided to find out what was in the box. She broke the lock and began to pry off the lid. She worked around the edges until the lid was loose. Gently she lifted the lid. Whoosh! She screamed and jumped back.

Out of the box flew all the horrors of the world — sickness, anger, envy, war, and poverty. They were all the things that make life difficult. Pandora realized her mistake and slammed the lid. But she was too late. She tried to catch the horrors, but they swirled through the window and out into the world forever. The only thing lying in the bottom of the box was Hope. It was all that was left to help troubled people during difficult times.

Main Idea
1. The most important thing about this story is
   a. the beauty of Pandora.
   b. the opening of the black box.
   c. Zeus' famous thunderbolt.

Significant Details
2. Who actually created Pandora?
   a. Hephaetus
   b. Zeus
   c. Achilles

Context Clues
3. They *swirled* through the window.
   a. twisted and turned
   b. creeped and crawled
   c. blew

Following Through
4. Do you think Hope was the best thing that could have been left for future people? Would something else have been better? Explain.

Curse of the Jade Tulip

Mike's cousin Andy was in town for the day and Mike was showing him his favorite spots. They had just finished a soda at the burger shop and were resting on the grass nearby.

"What's that big house across the street?" asked Andy.

"That belongs to a friend of mine, Mrs. Silverton — and her flowers. Guess what? She has a green tulip in her greenhouse and she says it has a curse on it," Mike said with a laugh. "Anyone who touches it will have a green hand for the rest of his life."

"I don't believe it," said Andy. "Show me."

The two boys went around the large house and back to the greenhouse door. No one was around and the door was open. They did not have to look far when they walked in. There on a table all by itself was a tulip with bright green petals. Slowly, Andy stretched his hand toward the tulip.

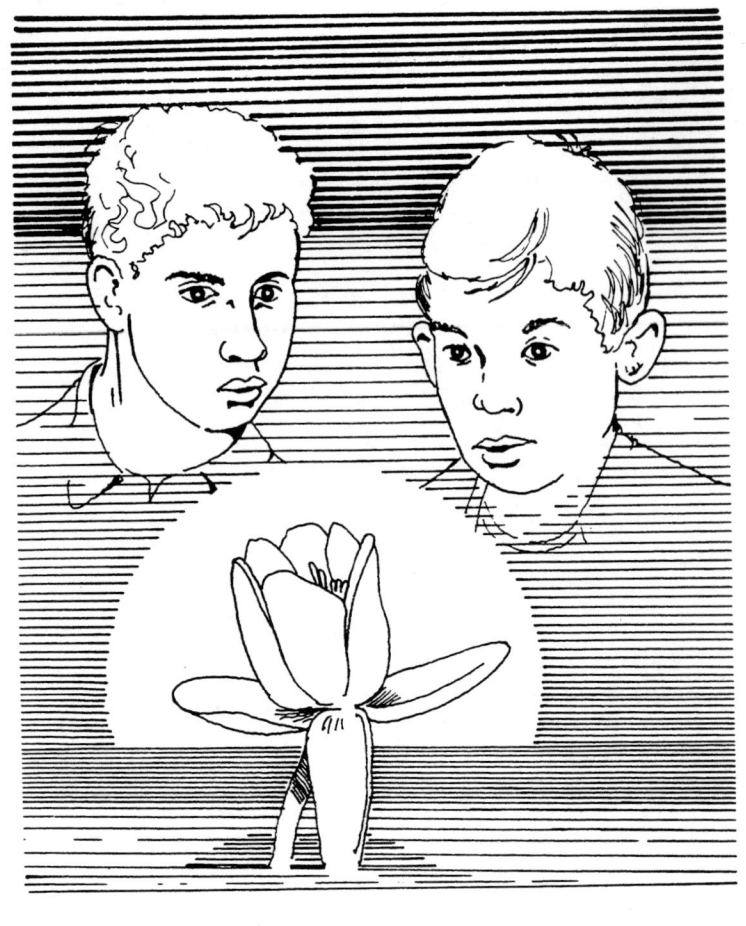

Finish the story. If necessary, continue on another paper.

The Clydesdales

The television ad flashes on and viewers watch as a pair of gates swing open. Through the gates rides a team of six magnificent horses pulling an old-fashioned delivery wagon. Two drivers and a dog are perched on top of the wagon. It is the famous Budweiser Clydesdales. In the early part of the century, August Busch, Jr., president of a midwest brewery and long time horse lover, put together the first Clydesdale "hitch." The hitch, or team, joined parades, carried presidents, and entered horse shows, all from its home base in St. Louis, Missouri. Today, the Clydesdales are national pets that travel all over the world. Thousands of requests are received each year for these powerful horses to appear at rodeos, benefits, and parades — even the Rose Bowl Parade!

Clydesdales, first bred in Scotland, are among the largest horses in the world. When they are full grown, they generally weigh over 2,000 pounds and are taller than a six-foot driver. They can eat fifty pounds of hay each day in addition to their regular feed. Basically, Clydesdales are workhorses with enough strength to plow or pull large loads all day. But their brisk leg action and white ankle "feathers," or hair, make them seem more graceful than other workhorses. With their gentle dispositions and handsome reddish coats, they make a smart appearance at any event.

The demand for such appearances has grown so fast that there are now two additional stables for hitches, one on the east coast and one on the west coast. The head driver of each hitch has many years of experience. He chooses new horses for his team with great care. The driver is the one responsible for seeing that all the preparations are made for an appearance. Horses are scrubbed, tails are braided, brass is polished, and leather harnesses are carefully fitted on the massive heads. Finally, grooms harness the horses to the wagon, the driver flicks the reins, and another Clydesdale show is on the road.

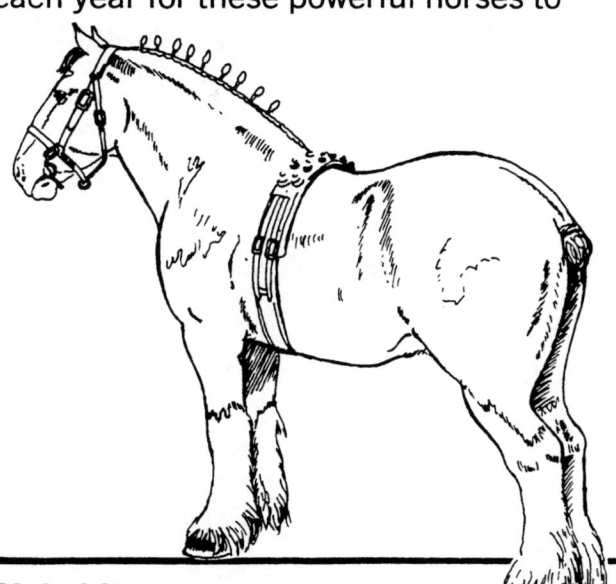

Main Idea
1. This story is mainly about
   a. the Rose Bowl Parade.
   b. unusual horses.
   c. Scottish stables.

Significant Details
2. How much hay can a grown Clydesdale eat each day?
   a. 2,000 pounds
   b. six feet
   c. fifty pounds

Context Clues
3. The word in paragraph three that is similar to *very large* is
   a. massive.
   b. braided.
   c. reins.

Inference
4. From the story, you can tell that the Clydesdales
   a. rest most of the year.
   b. like to be scrubbed.
   c. are busy most of the time.

Drawing Conclusions
5. Preparing the Clydesdales for a show requires
   a. about an hour.
   b. a lot of people.
   c. three drivers.

Following Through
6. Read about other kinds of horses such as the Tennessee walking horse or the quarter horse. Write a brief history of the development of one kind of horse.

The Trojan Horse
(Adapted from *The Aeneid*, an epic poem by Virgil)

Troy was a large, wealthy city on the coast of Turkey. According to mythology, Paris, a prince of Troy, kidnapped the beautiful Helen, who was the wife of a Greek king. The Greeks were very angry and organized an army to sail after Paris and bring Helen back. For ten years, the Greeks waged war against the city of Troy, but could not break down its defenses. Many heroes, on both sides, were killed and it seemed as if the war would last forever. Then, the Greeks thought of a plan.

They built a huge wooden horse and told everyone that this horse was to be an offering to the goddess Minerva for the safe return of Helen and their army. The Greeks seemed to be giving up as they boarded their ships and sailed away. The people of Troy opened their gates and rushed out to enjoy the freedom. There stood the horse.

Although a wise man told the Trojan people to have nothing to do with the Greek horse, they were excited and paid no attention. They brought the great horse into the city and continued to celebrate.

Late that night, a band of Greek soldiers, who had hidden inside the horse, crept out and unlocked the gates of the city. The Greek ships had not gone far. They had been lying in wait offshore and returned at dark. Many Greek soldiers now slipped into the city, and soon, were killing and burning everything in sight. Aeneas, one of the Trojan heroes, fought bravely, but it was no use. As the flames from his burning city lit the sky, Aeneas gathered a group of exiles and prepared to leave his homeland. Aeneas and his band wandered for years before they landed in Italy and founded the city of Rome.

Main Idea
1. The Trojans and the Greeks were
   a. at war.
   b. neighbors.
   c. in partnership.

Significant Details
2. According to the story, the fighting began because
   a. the Greeks wanted to rule Troy.
   b. Paris had killed a Greek soldier.
   c. a Greek woman was kidnapped.

Context Clues
3. The word *exiles* in the last paragraph means
   a. people forced to leave their homes.
   b. people wanting to fight.
   c. people who liked the Greeks.

Inference
4. From the story, you can tell that the Greeks were
   a. ready to give up.
   b. clever.
   c. a group of exiles.

Drawing Conclusions
5. The story leads you to believe that the huge Trojan horse was
   a. an offering to Helen.
   b. a cover for the Greek soldiers.
   c. a gift to the people of Troy.

Following Through
6. For centuries, Virgil has been considered one of the best Roman epic poets. Read about his life and write a brief biography.

Space Camp

For many years, young people have attended soccer or basketball camp during vacations to improve their skills. In 1982 an exciting working camp was added to the list — the U.S. Space Camp near Huntsville, Alabama. Huntsville, where the favorite phrase is "the sky is *not* the limit," is the location of NASA's Space and Rocket Center. It is also where the Redstone rocket that boosted the first astronauts into space was made. It is a good place for future astronauts to learn about space travel.

Campers may begin by building a rocket model. Later they discover how an astronaut trains. Sit-ups and jogging become part of their routine. Then there are full simulated shuttle missions with launching, handling, and landing practice. For several hours a "crew" will check controls, read instruments, and perform all tasks done by astronauts in flight. They will not actually leave the ground, but they will feel weightless, make decisions, and handle possible in-flight emergencies.

Although the program is non-profit, there is a fee for the camper's five-day stay. This includes food, lodging, and supplies. There are programs for students from the fourth grade through college level, and also for teachers.

In 1988, camp directors expected to work with over 18,000 students. And a new space camp near Cape Kennedy in Florida will make room for more. All campers may not wish to become astronauts. Some wish to do research; others want to become part of ground crews. But camp directors are sure that from these camping experiences will come many of the country's future astronauts.

Main Idea
1. The story tells about
   a. space travel.
   b. space shuttles.
   c. space training.

Significant Details
2. The first U.S. Space Camp is
   a. in Alabama.
   b. at Cape Kennedy.
   c. built on the moon.

Context Clues
3. Which word in paragraph two means about the same as "blast off?"
   a. simulated
   b. weightless
   c. launching

Inference
4. Campers have some interest in
   a. playing instruments.
   b. science.
   c. exercise.

Drawing Conclusions
5. This story leads us to believe
   a. more camps will be built.
   b. there are not many campers.
   c. more students will become astronauts.

The New Wheel

Jill was skillful at fixing things. She needed to be! The wheel on her bicycle was ruined and she really could not afford a new one. At Mr. Hooley's Junk Shop, she had found an old one for two dollars. The poor thing wobbled wildly as she rolled it home. It took forever, but she finally made it. Leaning the dented wheel against the garage, Jill went into the house for dinner.

Later, just as it was growing dark, Jill remembered the abandoned wheel. She ran out to put it into the garage for the night. As she approached the side of the garage, Jill saw a strange glow. It was coming from the wheel. As she moved closer, she heard a humming sound. Suddenly, the light grew brighter and the wheel began to roll toward her.

Finish the story. If necessary, continue on another paper.

Margaret Bourke-White

Margaret Bourke-White was only a sophomore in college when people began to recognize her unusual abilities with a camera. She was studying to be a biologist, but when her father died, she had to look for a way to support herself. Margaret began to take photos of familiar scenes on and near her college campus. At Christmas, she set up a booth and sold every shot she had taken.

After graduation, Margaret went to New York and succeeded in getting work with an architect. Very quickly, she became known for her talent in making bridges, factories, and other buildings look interesting. Margaret then began developing as a great photojournalist — a person who can tell a sad or happy story with a photo. With stark realism, she photographed the faces of those caught in the 1929 Depression. She toured the South and collected enough shots for a book about the poverty she saw there.

LIFE magazine sent her to Europe during World War II. The assignment began an exciting episode in her life. Bourke-White photographed heads of state, survivors of torpedoed ships, and prisoners of war. Finally, she got permission to fly on a bombing mission. Her plane was hit twice, but the pilot got "Maggie" and her photos safely back to base. Soon the young woman in a flight suit with a camera slung over her shoulder was a familiar sight along the battle routes.

Margaret had faced all kinds of discomfort. She had been to impossible places on improbable missions. But her last assignment was the most difficult. She contracted Parkinson's disease. She underwent surgery twice, and continued to fight the disease with all her power. Doctors were amazed at her courage. But not the soldiers, who had seen her with a smile on her face, waving to them in the middle of a shelling.

Main Idea
1. Margaret Bourke-White was
   a. a photojournalist.
   b. an architect of bridges.
   c. a biologist.

Significant Details
2. Margaret's book on the South shows people stricken by
   a. war.
   b. torpedoes.
   c. poverty.

Context Clues
3. In paragraph two, the word *stark* means
   a. clear.
   b. harsh.
   c. gentle.

Inference
4. The story suggests that
   a. people remember photographers a long time.
   b. people disliked Margaret during her life.
   c. Margaret overcame her disease.

Drawing Conclusions
5. From the story, you can conclude that Bourke-White was
   a. a sickly woman.
   b. a determined person.
   c. a lover of tragedy.

Following Through
6. Read more about Margaret Bourke-White's life. List places she visited and people she photographed.

St. Elmo's Fire

Long ago, those who sailed the Mediterranean Sea prayed to St. Elmo, the sailors' patron saint, for protection. Ships were often lost in bad weather and the crews hoped that St. Elmo would guide them to safety. But who knew whether or not the saint heard their prayers? One dark, stormy night, a sailor standing on a tossing deck looked up through the storm to the top of the masts. There he saw a strange, glowing light.

"Ahoy," he shouted to his mates. "A sign from St. Elmo! St. Elmo's Fire." Since then, to the sailors, this light has always meant a sure sign of their patron's protection.

What that sailor and others after him saw did look like fire. But how could flames spontaneously appear on top of a mast, especially in a fierce downpour? The sailors were mistaken. What they imagined to be St. Elmo's Fire was not fire at all. It was a strange, atmospheric phenomenon. The flash of light can be caused by a charge of electricity in the air. The true name for this phenomenon is *corona discharge*. It is a type of electrical conduction that usually occurs from pressure in the atmosphere's gases. A strong electric field, like a thunderstorm, is needed to produce the discharge. Along with the spectacular glow of light, there is a hissing sound.

St. Elmo's Fire is almost always seen around the masts of ships. But it has also

been noticed on top of other tall or projecting objects, such as church steeples, tree tops, or the tips of aircraft wings. It has even been seen around cattle's horns, horses' manes, and people's heads.

Modern sailors, who have observed the phenomenon, say that on a dark night, the round flash of colored light that is St. Elmo's Fire is quite a sight to remember.

Main Idea
1. The story is mainly about
    a. ghosts.
    b. an electrical phenomenon.
    c. sea stories.

Significant Details
2. Another name for St. Elmo's Fire is
    a. the patron saint.
    b. Mediterranean fire.
    c. corona discharge.

Context Clues
3. In paragraph three, the word *phenomenon* means
    a. an unusual event.
    b. sickness.
    c. myth.

Inference
4. From the story, you can tell that
    a. there must be many stories of St. Elmo's Fire.
    b. no one talked about it.
    c. most ships used to sink.

Drawing Conclusions
5. The story leads one to conclude that sailors today
    a. are still frightened by the fire.
    b. understand what causes the fire.
    c. have a new patron saint.

Following Through
6. Research northern lights and other atmospheric occurrences. What role does electricity play in these events?

Moby Dick
(Adapted from Herman Melville's novel)

One cold, Christmas morning the ship *Pequod* set sail from Nantucket. The crew, which included several harpooners, had not been told their ship's destination. Nor had the captain appeared. Later, when the ship reached warmer waters, the captain, Ahab, was seen standing on the deck, his peg leg anchored into a hole bored into the floor.

The captain then ordered the crew to assemble. He told them that the sole purpose of the journey was to hunt for the Great White Whale, Moby Dick. The captain had a deep desire for revenge on the whale that had taken his leg. Ahab called on the crew to help him find this vicious beast. The crew accepted the challenge and drank a pledge. In fact, they drank, shouted, and sang for the rest of the night.

The ship continued south and Ahab pored over his charts. He constantly asked passing ships for news of the whale. Then one day, a typhoon struck the ship with terrible force. Thunder and lightning raged and huge waves washed over the deck. In the midst of the storm, the sailors saw a strange glow on the tips of the three masts. The men were frightened by the eerie light, but the captain saw it as a sign of success.

And, shortly after the storm blew over, Ahab saw the whale at last.

For three days, the harpooners drove their weapons into the great animal. Moby Dick just shook them off and grew more and more angry. At last, Ahab, alone in his boat, harpooned the whale. But he got entangled in the rope. The captain, and finally all of the crew, were lost, except for one man, Ishmael, the storyteller, who was left to tell the tale.

Main Idea
1. The story tells about
   a. a peg leg.
   b. a search for a whale.
   c. the many voyages of the *Pequod*.

Significant Details
2. The storyteller of this sea story is
   a. Ishmael.
   b. Moby Dick.
   c. Ahab.

Context Clues
3. Which word in paragraph two means about the same as *getting even*?
   a. revenge
   b. vicious
   c. assemble

Inference
4. Reread the story *St. Elmo's Fire*, page 13. What event in this story describes the phenomenon of St. Elmo's Fire?
   a. A typhoon struck with terrible force.
   b. A strange glow of light was seen on the tips of the three masts.
   c. The harpooners drove their weapons into the whale.

Drawing Conclusions
5. In the end,
   a. Ahab got his revenge.
   b. Moby Dick got away.
   c. only three sailors survived.

Following Through
6. Read the novel *Moby Dick* by Herman Melville. Describe another adventure the crew encountered on the trip.

© Milliken Publishing Company

Ian Fleming

Ian Lancaster Fleming always had a taste for adventure. Born in 1908 in England, Ian was the second son in the wealthy Fleming family. He was educated at the finest schools. When he was twenty-one, Fleming took a job as a news correspondent in Moscow. Ian loved this job. He learned to speak Russian and was introduced to many fascinating people. Although Moscow offered plenty of adventures, the outbreak of World War II brought the biggest chance yet for an exciting life.

Back in London, Fleming served as personal assistant to the Director of British Naval Intelligence. He was given the rank of commander and put in charge of "special duties." Not many people knew what was involved in this job. Ian worked with secret codes and machines. He helped with top priority war plans. Traveling around the world, he met with undercover agents and spies.

Much of Ian Fleming's "special duties" still remain secret. But you can get a glimpse of his wartime job if you read the James Bond thriller series.

As an author, Ian Fleming created James Bond, the fictional Secret Agent 007. Fleming wrote a number of these spine-tingling, cloak-and-dagger James Bond adventures after the war. *Dr. No, Goldfinger, The Spy Who Loved Me, For Your Eyes Only*, and *Moonraker*, are a few of the books that brought Fleming success. Through them all, James Bond is seen as the daring, exciting, and seemingly untouchable secret agent who treks around the world on dangerous missions. Although Fleming claims that James Bond is a made-up character, many people who knew Ian personally say that he and James Bond are one and the same.

Indeed, there are many similarities between Ian and his fictional character. As a secret agent, James Bond was assigned the code name 007. Ian Fleming also operated under a code name, M, while working for the Naval Intelligence. The author does admit that most of his ideas for the James Bond series were based on things that actually happened to him while working for the British Intelligence.

For instance, while in Munich, Ian had a terrible car accident. He changed this real-life accident into a railway accident in which the villain, Scaramanga, was killed in *Man With a Golden Gun*.

Another time, Fleming was gambling in a casino in Portugal when he spotted German agents. Fleming thought he could halt the agents by taking all their money. Slyly, he enticed the men to bet in a casino game. In the end, Fleming was the one who lost all his money and the German agents escaped. But Ian had his revenge! In his book, *Casino Royale*, Ian puts James Bond in the same gambling game against an evil Communist official. This time, Bond was the winner and the Communist was in ruins.

Although Ian Fleming and James Bond share a love of gambling, fast cars, travel, and excitement, Fleming draws the line at violence. Bond is involved in many bloody killings, while Fleming hates killing of any kind.

With his writing, it seems that Ian Fleming may have found his best adventure of all. He was able to live out his exciting dreams through the heroic character of Agent 007, James Bond.

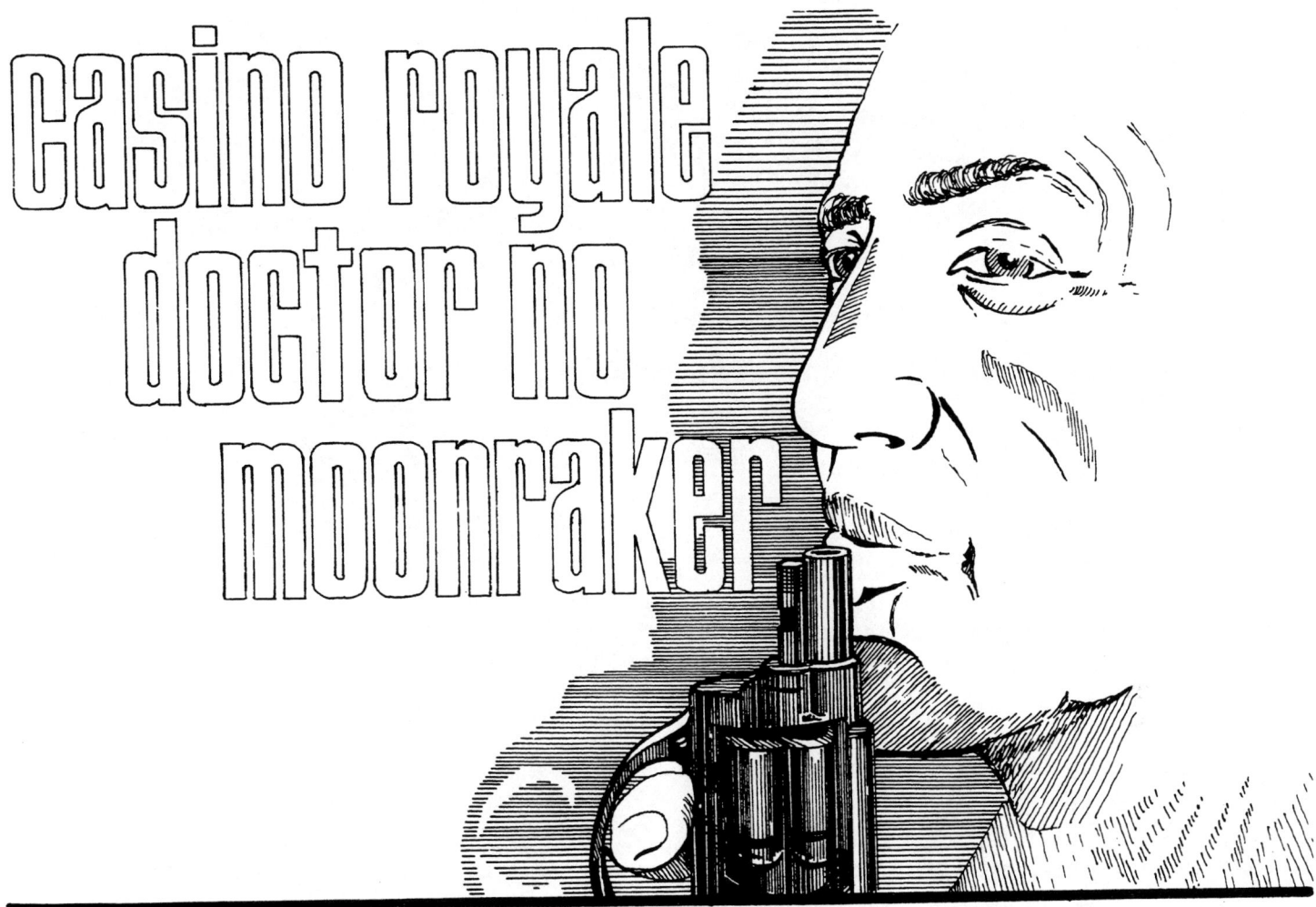

casino royale
doctor no
moonraker

Main Idea
1. This story is mainly about
   a. a World War II spy.
   b. an adventure in Moscow.
   c. a bad car accident in Munich.

Significant Details
2. Fleming created the fictional secret agent named
   a. Goldfinger.
   b. James Bond.
   c. "M."

Context Clues
3. In paragraph two, the word *priority* means
   a. most dangerous.
   b. hand-delivered.
   c. of most importance.

Inference
4. From the story, you would think Fleming was
   a. shy.
   b. daring.
   c. slow.

Drawing Conclusions
5. Fleming had to keep the secrets from World War II days because
   a. he did not remember the stories.
   b. he had lost important files.
   c. other people still alive could have been in danger.

Following Through
6. Read about the life of another adventurous author. John Le Carre, like Fleming, was a spy and now writes about undercover life. Write about events in the writer's real life that could make exciting reading.

Sports Medicine

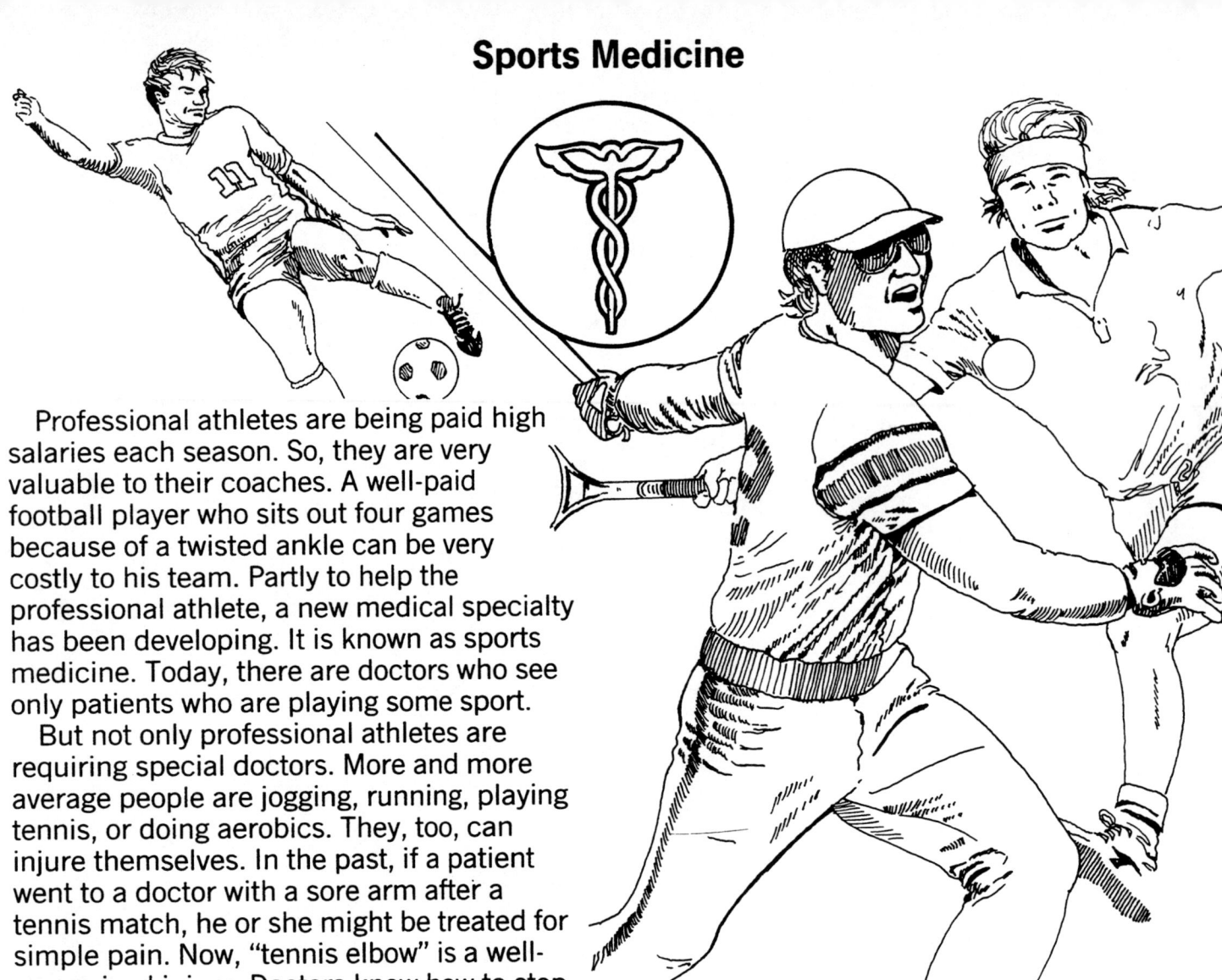

Professional athletes are being paid high salaries each season. So, they are very valuable to their coaches. A well-paid football player who sits out four games because of a twisted ankle can be very costly to his team. Partly to help the professional athlete, a new medical specialty has been developing. It is known as sports medicine. Today, there are doctors who see only patients who are playing some sport.

But not only professional athletes are requiring special doctors. More and more average people are jogging, running, playing tennis, or doing aerobics. They, too, can injure themselves. In the past, if a patient went to a doctor with a sore arm after a tennis match, he or she might be treated for simple pain. Now, "tennis elbow" is a well-recognized injury. Doctors know how to stop its pain and prevent its return.

Doctors who practice sports medicine are just as interested in preventing injuries and illness as in curing them. These specialists advise patients on how to avoid harmful exercising and over-training. They develop tests to measure how much stress a particular sport can cause a knee, an arm, or an ankle. Special nutrition goals are set for each sport. When does a swimmer eat a big meal? How long before a game does a ball player need protein? Even weather conditions are part of a sports doctor's studies. Hot weather requires different precautions and clothing than cold weather. And if, in spite of all efforts, an athlete does get hurt, the doctor will not only treat the injury, but also tell how long the player must rest, and whether or not the sport can still be played by the injured athlete.

Some doctors offer elaborate services, while others offer very simple services. One doctor has a huge truck trailer equipped as a gym. This trailer travels with athletes on some professional golf tours. Golfers may work out on the equipment between matches. For average athletes, some cities have opened diagnostic centers. One city even has a free hot line that will answer any emergency questions about an athletic injury. Now that we're prepared, let the games begin!

Main Idea
1. This story tells about
   a. new sports.
   b. tennis matches.
   c. special doctors.

Significant Details
2. Today, more average people are
   a. playing professional football.
   b. participating in athletic activities.
   c. becoming doctors.

Context Clues
3. The word *elaborate* in paragraph four means
   a. very complete and detailed.
   b. very elegant and expensive.
   c. emergency.
4. In a *diagnostic* center, you would
   a. get a high-protein meal.
   b. train on sports equipment.
   c. find out the nature of a sports injury.

Inference
5. You can tell from the story that sports doctors probably do not
   a. weigh their patients.
   b. remove tonsils.
   c. give medicine.

Drawing Conclusions
6. A sports doctor might regularly advise patients on
   a. how much sleep they need.
   b. where to buy the best gym clothes.
   c. how fast a truck can be driven.

Following Through
7. Check the telephone directory in your town and see if you have a sports diagnostic center or a free hot line. Try to interview a doctor in your area who practices sports medicine. The American Orthopedic Society is one place that lists such doctors.

Lorraine Hansberry

When Lorraine Hansberry was still in her twenties, she became a famous writer. In an interview, a reporter asked Hansberry why so many modern black writers were young. Lorraine answered, "Maybe because we have so much to say, we start earlier."

Lorraine did have plenty to say. But it took her some time to find the right method for saying it. Hansberry was born in Chicago and went to high school there. Next, she studied for two years at the University of Wisconsin. There, like many before her, she fell in love with the stage. However, she did not choose to be an actress. She was far more interested in writing for the stage. Lorraine also spent time studying art, but finally decided she had no real talent for the visual arts.

Searching for the right way to tell her story, Lorraine went to New York. Here, she began to write short stories and plays, but never finished most of them. To support herself, she worked as a reporter, as a clerk, and as a cashier at a restaurant owned by a family that published music. Through the job as cashier, Lorraine met Robert Nemiroff, the son of her employer. They married and moved into a Greenwich Village apartment. There Lorraine spent nearly a year writing a play. She and her husband read it to friends. Their response was enthusiastic. Within a year, that play, *Raisin in the Sun,* opened at the Barrymore Theater on Broadway. The drama told of the life and struggles of a black family in Chicago. Through her characters, Lorraine was able to show the inner and outer feelings of the family, as well as the courage with which they met the challenges of both old and new ways.

The play's title was taken from the poem *Harlem* by Langston Hughes, which asks: "What happens to a dream deferred? Does it dry up like a raisin in the sun. . . Does it explode?"

Lorraine's view of the world certainly exploded on the audience. *Raisin in the Sun* was the first play written by a black woman to be produced on Broadway. It became a smash success, and has traveled throughout the country. Although her promising start was cut short by an early death, Lorraine had found a way to share her vision.

Main Idea
1. The story tells about
   a. a struggling black family.
   b. a restaurant reporter.
   c. the success of a young playwright.

Significant Details
2. Lorraine grew up in
   a. Wisconsin.
   b. Chicago.
   c. Greenwich Village.

Context Clues
3. Which word in paragraph three means almost the same as *full of excitement?*
   a. challenges
   b. enthusiastic
   c. searching

Inference
4. *Raisin in the Sun* was a successful play because the playwright wrote
   a. from experiences close to her own life.
   b. about unusual people.
   c. about people ready to learn black history.

Drawing Conclusions
5. If Hansberry had lived, she would have
   a. begun to write comedies.
   b. become an actress.
   c. written more exciting plays.

Following Through
6. Read *Raisin in the Sun* by Lorraine Hansberry. Explain why the line from Langston Hughes' poem *Harlem* made a good title for this play.

The Sherpa

Have you ever wondered what it would be like to live in the land of the Abominable Snowman? The Sherpa, a tribe of hardy mountaineers, could tell you. Originally from Tibet, the Sherpa now live in the high regions of the country of Nepal. The country's northeast border runs along the Himalayas, where stands Mount Everest, the highest mountain in the world. High winds, avalanches, bitter cold, steep mountainsides, and plenty of snow make this part of the world very difficult to reach. The Sherpa are used to living at high altitudes and manage to farm and raise livestock. However, the occupation for which the Sherpa are world-famous is that of mountain guide. In fact, the name *Sherpa* has become synonymous with *guide*.

Outside groups and individuals frequently try to climb to the peak of Mount Everest. Without the help of the Sherpa, traveling in these mountains would be impossible. Since the Sherpa trade with other tribes across the mountains, they know the easiest of the steep paths. They can give advice on the best type of clothing to wear and the most important supplies to pack. Because the ground is so rough and hilly, pack animals would be of no use on such an expedition. Instead, the Sherpa carry on their backs all the needed supplies. For this reason, the Sherpa must have strong bodies. In 1953, after more than two months of climbing, Sir Edmund Hillary of New Zealand, and his Sherpa guide, Tenzing Norgay, became the first persons on record to reach the top of Mount Everest.

The Sherpa, along with the other people of Nepal, practice a combination of Hinduism and Buddhism. Influenced by nearby Tibet, Buddhist monks, called lamas, guide their strong beliefs. Western mountain climbers find their guides to be of high character, reliable, and filled with a sense of humor. In the Sherpa code, tolerance and compassion for others rank very high. All of these combine to make a Sherpa a good person to have at one's side in the middle of a mountain blizzard.

Main Idea
1. This story is mainly about
   a. raising livestock in the mountains.
   b. an interesting people.
   c. the teachings of the high lama.

Significant Details
2. The New Zealand climber who mastered Mount Everest in 1953 was
   a. Tenzing Norgay.
   b. the high lama.
   c. Edmund Hillary.
3. The Sherpa learned about the best paths by
   a. studying maps.
   b. crossing the mountains for trade.
   c. passing down stories.

Context Clues
4. The word *synonymous* means
   a. about the same as.
   b. Sherpan for guide.
   c. short for guess.

Inference
5. From what you have read, you would guess that high mountain climbs would take
   a. several months.
   b. several days.
   c. several hours.

Drawing Conclusions
6. The story leads you to conclude that the Sherpa have links with the people of
   a. New Zealand.
   b. Tibet.
   c. China.

Following Through
7. Study a world map. Find Nepal and Mount Everest. How high is this mountain? Read about high mountains in the United States. Which ones are popular with mountain climbers? Do these climbers use guides?

© Milliken Publishing Company

The Mountain Lion
(Adapted from a Tibetan tale)

Long ago, a widow and her two sons lived on a small farm in a valley of Tibet. All around them were beautiful, soaring mountains. The family was very poor and the boys did what they could to earn money. The older boy was quick and smart, while the younger was slow and kind. The older boy did more work, but the younger one tried very hard to keep up with his brother.

One day, the older brother grew angry when his brother could not fill a water trough fast enough to suit him. "I have had enough," he said. "I work hard all day to raise money to buy us food, and you just poke along. I am tired of taking care of you. You must leave here and learn how to take care of yourself."

Sadly, the younger brother packed to leave. When his mother discovered what had happened, she decided to leave, too. She preferred kindness to smartness. So, the kind, slow son and his mother began to look for a new home. They had not gone very far when they found an empty cabin. It was at the base of a high mountain. The two decided to spend the night in the cabin and the boy would look for work in the morning. The next day, the boy woke early and found an ax near the back door. He chopped wood all morning, hauled the logs to a nearby town, and sold them. It was a beginning.

The next morning the boy went up the mountain in search of more wood. He stumbled into a clearing, and there before him was a large lion. The boy stood very still. But the lion did not move. At last, the boy realized that the beast was made of stone. He thought that the great stone creature must be the god of the mountain, so he wished to offer it a gift. The boy searched his pockets and found a candle stub. Hastily, he brushed it off and set it before the lion. As he lit the candle, he bent his head and said, "Thank you, oh mighty lion, for helping me to find work."

To his great surprise, the lion spoke. "Who are you? What are you doing here in these woods?"

Quickly the boy told him where he was living and how he was trying to support his mother with money from selling wood. The lion listened patiently. Then, the great beast told the boy to bring a bucket with him the next time. That evening, the boy went down the mountain with a large bundle of wood. He sold it in town and returned to the cabin to tell his mother about the lion. The widow helped her son to find a bucket. The next morning, the boy returned to the clearing and knelt in front of the lion.

"I see you have obeyed me," said the lion. "Now, hold the bucket under my mouth and I will fill it with gold pieces. But you must not let one piece hit the ground. Say 'stop' before it overflows."

The boy held the bucket carefully and gold pieces poured into it. As they began to reach the rim, he said "stop" so that not one piece hit the ground. Once again he thanked the lion. Then he took the full bucket home to his mother. With the money, they were able to buy a large farm and lead a happy, prosperous life.

Main Idea
1. Which moral could sum up this story?
   a. The faster you work, the further you get.
   b. The gift of kindness is worth more than material gains.
   c. Don't count your chickens before they hatch.

Significant Details
2. The lion was
   a. stone.
   b. fierce.
   c. fast.

Context Clues
3. The word *prosperous* in the last paragraph means
   a. preposterous.
   b. short.
   c. filled with good things.

Inference
4. You can tell the story is fiction because
   a. brothers are never unkind to each other.
   b. wood cannot be sold.
   c. statues don't talk.

Drawing Conclusions
5. The mountain was important to the younger brother because
   a. its woods provided a way to earn a living.
   b. he loved the scenery.
   c. it was full of lions.

Following Through
6. Read other folk and fairy tales. Can you find other stories that have the same moral? Retell a story in which goodness is rewarded.

Toying with New Ideas

Elmer Ambrose Sperry, an inventor from New York, has created many things, including electric mining machinery and electric railways. He also developed the high-intensity lighting used for street lamps and searchlights. The idea for his best-known invention came from a simple toy. His children were spinning a top and wondered why the top could stand without falling over.

Their question started Sperry thinking. The gyroscope, a mechanical device which defies the force of gravity, is much like a child's spinning top. The gyroscope is basically a spinning wheel with an axle through the center. The wheel rotates on bearings within a moveable frame. Another child's toy, the bicycle, can also be compared to the gyroscope. The spinning wheels keep the bike upright. When the frame of the wheel is turned, the bike goes in the direction of the turn. Sperry thought this motion could be put to many good uses.

Sperry developed new uses for the gyroscope. First he made a large gyroscope to help steady ships and keep them from rolling from side to side. In 1908, Sperry used this same idea to invent the gyrocompass. Steel used in manufacturing ships interferes with magnetic compasses. The gyrocompass isn't affected by steel or other magnetic forces. Its needle always shows a true north. Sperry also developed gyroscopes for submarines and aerial torpedoes, which were used during World War I.

Sperry's son, Lawrence, took his father's idea even further. He developed an automatic gyropilot to stabilize airplanes. Lawrence demonstrated his gyropilot by taking his hands off the steering wheel of a flying airplane and walking out on the airplane's wing! Many fighting methods used by today's army and navy would not be possible without Sperry.

Main Idea
1. Elmer Sperry is best known for his development of
   a. electric mining machinery.
   b. airplanes.
   c. gyroscopes.

Significant Details
2. The gyrocompass is better than the magnetic compass because
   a. magnets on a magnetic compass point north.
   b. the gyrocompass is not affected by magnetic forces.
   c. the gyrocompass is bigger.

Context Clues
3. The gyropilot was used to *stabilize* airplanes.
   a. make steady
   b. manufacture
   c. fly without power

Inference
4. What did Lawrence prove by walking on the wing of an airplane?
   a. He was an experienced flyer.
   b. The plane could fly without gas.
   c. The gyroscope could keep the plane automatically on course.

The Birth of an Island

Most of the earth was formed millions of years ago. In centuries past, explorers ventured into unknown lands until every corner of the world had been searched and charted on maps.

But modern explorers had a chance in recent years to roam about a new land formation off the coast of Iceland. In fact, in November 1963, some local fishermen actually saw the new island being formed—by the eruption of a volcano!

The hot, molten lava of the volcano cooled and settled after a few weeks. During this time, an island over a mile long and 567 feet high was created. The new island is called Surtsey, after a fairy tale giant. Although people were not eager to move their homes to Surtsey, the birds were. Local birds carrying seeds from plants on Iceland flocked to the island. Within a few years, the first flower bloomed. Soon over twenty kinds of plants and mosses were growing on the island.

The people were wise not to build homes on Surtsey. Already the ocean currents are wearing away bits of this lava island. No one knows how long Surtsey will be able to withstand the strong waters of the North Atlantic Ocean.

Main Idea
1. Surtsey was formed
   a. millions of years ago.
   b. by a giant.
   c. by a volcano.

Significant Details
2. The island was formed by
   a. hot, molten lava.
   b. local fishermen.
   c. ocean currents.

Context Clues
3. Countries were *charted* on maps.
   a. seen
   b. placed
   c. discovered
4. Explorers *ventured* into strange lands.
   a. covered with paint
   b. refused to go
   c. went in spite of danger

Inference
5. Why might it not be safe on Surtsey?
   a. There are too many birds.
   b. The island may be washed away.
   c. Crops cannot grow in the lava.

6. Surtsey was created
   a. over twenty-five years ago.
   b. over two hundred years ago.
   c. in 567.

Drawing Conclusions
7. Would it be possible to see another island being formed somewhere in the ocean?
   a. Yes. Another volcano could erupt, leaving a lava island.
   b. Yes, people may build a new one.
   c. No, all of the earth's formations are already in place.

Following Through
8. Research other islands which have been formed by volcanoes. How long have they lasted? Do people inhabit them? _____

9. Find out about Surtsey, the fairy tale giant. Why do you think this island was named for him? _____

The Spectre Bridegroom
(Adapted from *The Sketch Book*, by Washington Irving)

A wealthy German baron had only one child, a beautiful girl. The baron had arranged a good marriage for his daughter with Count von Altenberg, the son of a nobleman. Everyone at the baron's castle was preparing for the bridegroom's arrival.

The count and his servants were on their way to the wedding when they met Herman von Starkenfaust. Herman was an old friend who had just returned from the army. The two friends rode on ahead. They had much to talk about. Suddenly they were attacked by bandits. When the servants arrived, they were too late to help. The wounded count was dying. He asked his friend to break the news to his bride-to-be and her father.

Herman put on black mourning clothes and sadly rode on to the castle. The baron greeted him eagerly, thinking he was the bridegroom. He gave Herman no chance to deliver his sad news. When Herman saw the bride-to-be, he immediately fell in love with her. He decided on a plan.

At midnight he rose to leave. Herman explained in a hollow voice that he had to lay his head elsewhere that night. Dressed in black and riding a black horse, Herman rode away into the night. The next day the count's servants brought the news that the bridegroom had been killed. It must have been a ghost, or spectre, who had come to the castle.

But the daughter knew better. Secretly she met Herman. They rode away and were married. Everyone thought she had been stolen by a spectre. Then one day a handsome knight and his lady arrived at the castle. The baron saw that it was his daughter and the spectre bridegroom. The spectre was really a fine, young nobleman, fit for his daughter. Although it was not the marriage he had wanted, the baron gave his blessing to the happy couple.

Main Idea
1. The beautiful daughter married
   a. Count von Altenberg.
   b. a German baron.
   c. Herman von Starkenfaust.

Context Clues
2. He wore *mourning* clothes.
   a. before lunch
   b. showing sorrow
   c. torn

Inference
3. How do you know the baron and the count had never met?
   a. The baron thought Herman was the count.
   b. The count lived in another country.
   c. The count introduced himself when he arrived at the castle.

Treetop Balloons

Hot-air balloons have been used for many reasons. They make weather observations and test equipment in high altitudes. Hot-air balloon races have become very popular. Balloons have even been used to study the atmosphere of Venus.

But now a Frenchman, Dr. Francis Halle, has found a new use for the hot-air balloon. Dr. Halle is doing a treetop study of a rain forest in South America. He is using a balloon platform to do it.

Dr. Halle is a botanist. A botanist is a person who studies plant life. Like many other botanists, Halle was upset because he could not examine the richest part of the forest. It is called the treetop canopy. His idea was to land a hot-air balloon on top of the trees to gather samples to study.

Getting the balloon to land evenly on the treetops, 160 feet above the ground, was very tricky. But once the platform was safely in place, the balloon was deflated, and scientists began their work. A large fan will help the crew inflate the balloon when the study is finished.

The scientists walk on the edge of the platform with safety lines attached to their waists. In this way, they are able to gather unusual leaves, flowers, fruits, and insects. Most of these things had not been studied before because they could not be reached. Dr. Halle feels his treetop work is very important. With new roads and other progress, large parts of the rain forest may be wiped out. Inhabitants of the forest may be endangered. Dr. Halle hopes that his treetop balloon study will help save some of the plants and animals of the rain forest.

Main Idea
1. How is the treetop balloon helpful?
   a. It proves that balloons can safely be landed on treetops.
   b. It allows people to study nature's hard-to-reach areas.
   c. It proves that the French have the most knowledge of balloons.

Significant Details
2. The richest part of the rain forest is
   a. the top part of the trees.
   b. the thick, dark soil.
   c. the plants and shrubs.

Context Clues
3. *Inhabitants* of the rain forest
   a. build roads through the forest.
   b. live in the forest.
   c. study in the forest.

Inference
4. How can Dr. Halle's work save the plants and animals of the rain forest?
   a. The road builders will stop their work when they see the balloon.
   b. The way plants and animals live and grow can be studied.
   c. People will donate money to Dr. Halle for research.

Drawing Conclusions
5. Dr. Halle is probably a resourceful man because
   a. he studies plants.
   b. he was the first man to fly a balloon in South America.
   c. he invented a new and practical use for the balloon.

Dogs That Make A Difference

When Toby, a large collie dog, places a dollar bill on the check-out counter at the supermarket, he is not asking for dog biscuits. He is helping his master, who cannot reach the counter. Toby is one of the support dogs being trained to make life easier for some handicapped people.

For many years dogs have been faithful helpers to the blind. But more and more of them will be seen in the future as helpers for people with spinal, back, muscle, or other problems that make movement difficult. For example, Toby's master has multiple sclerosis. If he should fall, Toby moves close and stands firmly so the man can pull himself upright. Toby can also open doors, pick up money and clothes off the floor, and bring the phone to his master.

Dogs used in this program are generally large breeds such as Great Danes, Labradors, golden retrievers, and German shepherds. In one city, 24 Labrador puppies will soon go into training. They will live with a foster family for about a year. The more activity in the family, the better. Then the puppies begin a nine-month training program. They learn to pull wheelchairs up ramps, open heavy glass mall doors, pick up canes, crutches, or other articles that have been dropped. Not all of the dogs will be capable of performing these activities. Those that cannot are then sent back to their foster families to be loved as pets. But most can be trained to help make life easier for someone who needs them.

These dogs have totally changed the lives of many handicapped people who were afraid to go out alone. Now these people have confidence in themselves. Family members of the handicapped often worry about leaving them alone at home. They are less anxious about leaving when a reliable dog is on duty. The dog and his master or mistress form a trusting and loving bond. For many people, a support dog has made life pleasant again.

Main Idea
1. This story is mainly about
   a. Labradors.
   b. wheelchairs.
   c. support dogs.

Significant Details
2. Toby can
   a. open doors.
   b. ring up the cash register.
   c. talk on the phone.
3. Before training begins, puppies
   a. stay at the kennel.
   b. live with a foster family.
   c. must be ten days old.
4. Which dog is suitable for the support program?
   a. German shepherd
   b. cocker spaniel
   c. dachshund

Drawing Conclusions
5. Larger dogs are used as support dogs because
   a. they scare away intruders.
   b. they can pull heavier weights and offer more support for someone to lean against.
   c. people can see them coming and will get out of their way.

The Rescuers

"All hands on deck," called the captain of the rescue boat. "Be on the lookout for survivors of the *Trawler!*"

The *Trawler* was a fishing boat which had been out to sea for a month. The boat was overdue. When it did not return, the rescue boat was sent to search for it. Eight men manned the rescue boat. Each one scanned the surface of the water with binoculars, hoping to see the fishing boat.

"We'd better turn back, Captain," said one of the men. "Our coal supply is very low. We have only enough fuel for one more day at sea."

"Very well," agreed the captain. "I thought we'd find the *Trawler* by now. We had better not take any chances."

As the rescue boat was turning homeward, a huge snowstorm arose. The wind howled, and the temperature dropped to freezing levels. No matter how hard the crew worked, the mighty storm pushed the boat further and further from shore. By nightfall, the coal supply was gone, and the rescue boat floated aimlessly in the winter storm. In the morning the crew awoke to find all their food frozen solid. Without coal for fire, there was no way to thaw the food. A few days passed, and the men got weaker and weaker.

Suddenly there was a shout. "Land ho! I see land!" Off in the distance they thought they saw a mountain range capped with snow. But the captain saw that it was really a huge iceberg! They were heading straight for it! He knew there was no hope for them now. The boat would crash, and they would all be killed.

Just then the captain heard, "Need any help?" It was the crew of the missing *Trawler*. They had been lost in the storm and were now returning home. Huge ropes were thrown from the *Trawler* to the rescue boat, and both boats moved away from the iceberg. A few days later, everyone on shore was delighted to see the *Trawler* pull into port with the rescue boat in tow.

Main Idea
1. Which boat had more difficulty?
    a. the rescue boat
    b. the *Trawler*
    c. the ocean liner

Significant Details
2. Why couldn't the rescue crew eat?
    a. Their food was gone.
    b. They only had fish.
    c. Their food was frozen.

Context Clues
3. They looked for *survivors*.
    a. fish
    b. people who escaped an accident
    c. binoculars

Inference
4. How do you think the captain felt when he saw the iceberg?
    a. thrilled to have found land
    b. excited to have seen an iceberg
    c. frightened

Drawing Conclusions
5. An event is ironic when the opposite of what is expected happens. What was ironic about this story?
    a. The *Trawler* was lost.
    b. The rescue boat was rescued.
    c. The captain recognized an iceberg.

Rudyard Kipling

In 1907, Rudyard Kipling became the first English writer to receive the Nobel prize for literature. Although he was an Englishman, much of his writing concerned India, a country that fascinated him. Kipling was born in Bombay, India, where his English father was the head of an art school. As a young child, Kipling learned to speak the Hindustani language of India. Kipling was sent to school in England. When he was seventeen, he came back to India and began writing.

Kipling thought India was a mysterious country and wrote stories that described its customs. He also liked to tell of the courage and skill of both English and Indian soldiers in battle. He wrote down many Indian folktales and even created some animal tales of his own. Any child who has read his *Just So Stories* will never forget how the leopard got its spots or how the elephant got its long trunk. Kipling's sense of humor can be found in many of his works.

When Kipling returned to England, he became an instant best-seller. His work was very popular with English readers. His prose was vivid, and many of his poems had such strong rhythm that they were set to music. Kipling married an American and lived on her estate in Vermont for a time. There he wrote a very famous book for young people, *The Jungle Book*. It is the story of the boy Mowgli, who is raised in the Indian jungle by friendly animals. Kipling became so popular in the United States that many towns were named for him.

Kipling made a foreign country come alive for his readers. He wrote a novel, *Kim*, an adventure story about an Indian orphan. It is a masterpiece that describes the interesting ways of India. Kipling continued to write about many subjects until his death in 1936.

Main Idea
1. What was Kipling's life work?
   a. animal keeper
   b. soldier
   c. writer

Significant Details
2. The story of Mowgli is told in
   a. verse.
   b. Hindustani.
   c. the *Jungle Book*.

Context Clues
3. Kipling's *masterpiece* tells of the interesting ways of India.
   a. only novel
   b. best work
   c. most expensive work

4. Kipling *created* animal tales.
   a. made up
   b. copied
   c. listened to

Drawing Conclusions
5. Although it does not say in the story, you can guess that Kipling
   a. was afraid of elephants.
   b. found Vermont cold.
   c. liked children.

Following Through
6. Check out a copy of *Just So Stories*. Read some of them. Choose one of the animals and write your own version of how the elephant got its trunk and how the hippo got its skin.

The Sacred Ganges

The Ganges River, one of the largest rivers in the world, flows through the center of India. The river provides fertile valleys throughout India, where many crops can be grown. Many of India's largest cities are located on the shores of the Ganges.

To the Hindus, members of one of India's largest religious groups, the river has a special meaning. They think the river is more than a source of water. They believe that the river is sacred.

An Indian legend says that long ago there was no river. During the droughts, the hot sun burned up the crops, and people began dying of hunger and thirst. A holy man prayed to the goddess Ganga and begged her for water. The goddess paid no attention to him. The determined holy man prayed again, this time standing on one leg. He stood in this position for a long time. Ganga admired this man's will power. Self-discipline and will power are highly respected in the Hindu religion. Ganga rewarded the man by coming to earth herself in the form of a river.

Many Hindus still believe that the Ganges River is a goddess. It is the wish of every Hindu to bathe at least once in the Ganges. Every year thousands of Hindus journey to the Ganges to bathe in its waters. People who live nearby bathe in the river every day before prayer time. According to the Hindu belief, those lucky enough to touch the waters of the Ganges are assured purity, wealth, and healthy children.

Main Idea
1. To Hindus, the Ganges is most important for its
    a. fertile valleys.
    b. sacred powers.
    c. trading centers.

Significant Details
2. Ganga was a
    a. holy man.
    b. Hindu.
    c. goddess.
3. A Hindu is
    a. a member of a religious group.
    b. a city on the Ganges.
    c. a river in India.

Context Clues
4. If you are *self-disciplined*, you
    a. live by yourself.
    b. earn your own money.
    c. have control over yourself.
5. During a *drought*, there is
    a. too much rain.
    b. no rain.
    c. too much snow.

Inference
6. From the story, you might guess that the water of the Ganges is
    a. good to drink.
    b. full of fish.
    c. dirty.

Captains Courageous
(Adapted from the novel by Rudyard Kipling)

Harvey Cheyne, a rich, spoiled young boy, was vacationing on a luxury ocean liner with his mother. One dark, foggy night Harvey fell overboard and was lost at sea. As he struggled to stay afloat in the rolling waves, Harvey thought he heard a voice. Suddenly a strong hand pulled him out of the cold water. He had been rescued by a fisherman from the boat *We're Here*. Harvey immediately ordered the crew to sail back to shore. He said his father was a millionaire and would reward them well. The crew just laughed. The boy begged them to return to land. He told them his father would come for him in his big automobile. Again the crew laughed. No one they knew owned his own car! Harvey offered them his monthly allowance — two hundred dollars. The men did not believe that Harvey was given that much money every month. In those days, ten dollars a month was a good wage for a fisherman.

The captain explained that since they were far out at sea, Harvey could not return home immediately. When the hold was full of fish, the ship would return to land. Harvey would have to work on the boat, along with the crew, to earn his food. Harvey was furious! He was rich and rich boys shouldn't have to do any work!

For months Harvey sailed on the *We're Here.* He learned very quickly that if he did not work, he did not eat. He also learned that boasting about money, servants, and all the things his family owned was not winning him any friends. These men admired hard work, not wealth.

Harvey learned how to man the rigging, tie the ropes, and drop the heavy anchor. Each day it was his job to pull up the dories, small rowboats that the men used to catch fish. Harvey also hauled in the day's catch and cleaned the fish. This was very hard, dirty work, especially for a spoiled boy who had never done chores before.

Harvey came to respect the sea and the hard-working men on the fishing boat. Harvey enjoyed listening to the crew members talk about their lives on the water, and the crew came to care about Harvey. They admired the way he learned things so quickly. They were pleased with his ability to work hard. Harvey was happy that he was finally with people who liked him for himself instead of his millions. He became a close friend of the captain's son, Dan, who was about the same age as Harvey. Dan was the only one who believed Harvey's stories about mansions, private

continued...

cars, and dinner parties. He even believed Harvey when he said his father owned many large ships.

Harvey did a lot of growing up on the ship. He worked as hard as the other fishermen and learned to take care of himself. When the ship finally returned home four months later, Harvey telegraphed his parents. A joyful Mr. and Mrs. Cheyne did indeed pick up Harvey in their own automobile. The crew was very surprised that Harvey's parents were actually millionaires. Harvey had mixed feelings. He was very happy to see his parents, but he knew he would miss the crew of the *We're Here*. They had taught him things about life and friendship that he would never forget. Harvey knew he would miss Dan the most. He had been such a good friend. When Mr. Cheyne heard all about Harvey's adventures on the fishing boat, he made Dan a mate on one of his fleet of ships.

Mr. and Mrs. Cheyne were thrilled to hear that their son was alive and well. They were delighted to see him. They could not believe how he had changed. They had lost a spoiled, selfish little boy. When he returned to them, he was a strong, caring young man.

Main Idea
1. Kipling's sea story is mostly about
   a. how the wealthy live.
   b. hard-working fishermen.
   c. the first automobile.

Significant Details
2. Part of Harvey's job was to
   a. serve dinner to the crew.
   b. sail the ship.
   c. load the fish onto the ship.
3. It was Dan who
   a. believed that Harvey was a millionaire's son.
   b. threw Harvey off the ship.
   c. made Harvey work so hard.

Context Clues
4. Ten dollars was a good *wage*.
   a. money earned for work
   b. allowance from parents
   c. money to buy fish
5. Harvey was *furious* when he was told he had to work.
   a. very happy
   b. very angry
   c. very scared
6. The *hold* was full of fish.
   a. space below the deck
   b. net
   c. pan

Inference
7. From the story, you can tell that most of the men on the ship probably led simple lives because
   a. they did not earn as much as Harvey earned.
   b. they were not impressed by money.
   c. none of them owned their own home.

Drawing Conclusions
8. Harvey did a lot of growing up on the ship. This probably meant that he
   a. was much taller at the end of the trip.
   b. had earned enough money to buy his own boat.
   c. had learned the importance of working hard.
9. Harvey and his family made sure Dan was treated well by giving him a good job on their fleet of ships. Why do you think they did this?
   a. The Cheyne's felt bad that Dan had to live so horribly, working as a fisherman.
   b. Dan told Harvey it was the least Harvey could do after all Dan and his father did for him.
   c. Dan was a good friend to Harvey and believed him when no one else did.

© Milliken Publishing Company

The Cobra

A guide is leading his party of visitors quietly through a forest in India. Suddenly he stops. On the path in front of him is a deadly cobra. It is as tall as he is. The front part of the snake's body is upright and swaying back and forth. It has spread the ribs of its long neck into a wide, flat "hood." Its tongue flicks in and out. The cobra, almost ten feet long, is ready to strike.

But the guide, who knows cobras well, knows that the cobra's strike is slower than the strike of some other snakes. So he knows that he has time to grab a stick and knock the cobra aside. The snake retreats into a tangle of tree roots.

Something must have disturbed the cobra because it does not hunt humans. It does not even attack large animals. But still it is one of the most feared and deadly of all snakes.

A cobra's hollow fangs carry poison that is five times more powerful than that of a rattlesnake. These fangs are only one fourth as long as a rattlesnake's. But once a cobra strikes, it continues to pump more and more venom into its prey. Some kinds of cobras can spray venom from their fangs into the eyes of a victim six feet away. The fangs are shaped so that the poison is "spit" forward when the cobra tilts back its head. The victim, usually a small animal, is blinded, and the cobra captures it easily. Most cobras eat many kinds of animals such as frogs, fish, birds, and other small mammals. Its spray is also a good defense against a large animal, such as a lion.

In spite of the cobra's ability to wound and kill, there are animals that can defeat the snake. In India, the small mongoose, a member of the weasel family, likes to steal and eat cobra eggs. The mongoose is fast enough to jump out of the way each time the mother cobra strikes. When the snake tires, the mongoose jumps in and bites the cobra

continued . . .

on the neck. In Africa, the strange secretary bird feeds on snakes. The bird is clever enough to let the snake strike harmlessly at its feathers. Then it tramples the snake. Africans sometimes keep tame secretary birds to protect them from the cobras. Eagles and other birds of prey sometimes kill and eat cobras, as well.

But if all cobras were killed, the natural balance of nature would be badly upset. In India alone, the rat population would overrun the country. It is now kept under control by the cobra.

India's jugglers and snake charmers use the cobra because of its unusual hood and nervous actions. They pretend to charm the snakes with their music, but in truth, the snakes would act the same way without the music. The cobras can only hear a limited range of sounds and cannot hear the music.

Main Idea
1. This story is mainly about
   a. the clever mongoose.
   b. the forests of India.
   c. a dangerous kind of snake.

Significant Details
2. Where is the cobra's poison carried?
   a. in its hood
   b. in its hollow fangs
   c. behind its eye
3. A cobra's hood is its
   a. flattened neck.
   b. poisonous tail.
   c. venomous fangs.

Context Clues
4. The snake's *venom* is the same as
   a. poison.
   b. attack.
   c. food.
5. Snakes hear a *limited* range of sounds.
   a. wide
   b. loud
   c. small

Inference
6. From the story, you can tell that
   a. Africa has rain forests.
   b. the cobra is more dangerous than the rattlesnake is.
   c. the cobra lives in treetops.
7. While the cobra looks like it is being "charmed," it is probably only
   a. holding itself on guard.
   b. listening to the music.
   c. doing what the charmer wants it to do.

Drawing Conclusions
8. From what you read about the cobra, you can guess that
   a. a person bitten by a cobra will probably die.
   b. people hunt the cobra for its valuable skin.
   c. cobras are found in all parts of the world.

© Milliken Publishing Company

The Smallest Warrior
(A retold Jataka tale)

Long ago in India there lived a small man who was a very skilled archer. He was probably the best bowman in India, but no one noticed him because he was so small. More than anything the small man wanted to join the king's army and use his archery skills to defend the king. But he thought that because of his small size he had no chance of being chosen by the king.

He decided to look for a large man to be his partner. The two would join the army as a team. The little man went to the city and found a big, strong man digging a ditch. The bowman explained his idea. The large man agreed to join him and divide a soldier's pay equally.

The king liked the large man and his little helper and hired them at once. He sent them off to battle on his biggest war elephant. Things worked well for a while. The king would send the large man out to battle, and the little man would go along to do his shooting. All the praise and rewards were given to the large man because eveyone thought he had done the work.

Then one day during a very fierce battle the large man lost his nerve. He was so afraid that he jumped from the war elephant and ran home. The little man had to go on alone. He charged into the battle, riding his war elephant, and began shooting at the enemy. Eventually, the enemy had enough of the little bowman and retreated. News of the victory was sent quickly to the king. When the small man returned, the king was waiting for him with praise and gifts. He received his greatest honor when the king made him the new chief of the army.

Main Idea
1. The little man in the story was successful because he
   a. deceived the king.
   b. used his skills.
   c. tamed a war elephant.

Significant Details
2. The story takes place in
   a. India.
   b. mountains.
   c. Egypt.
3. Who did the fighting in the story?
   a. the king
   b. the little man
   c. the large man

Context Clues
4. A skilled *archer*
   a. shoots a gun.
   b. trains elephants.
   c. shoots a bow and arrow.

Inference
5. The king will probably make different judgments in the future because he
   a. needs more bowmen in his army.
   b. lost the war.
   c. learned to judge a man by his skill.

Drawing Conclusions
6. Skill and courage do not depend on size and strength. This was proven when
   a. the king sent the large man to fight.
   b. the large man ran from the battle.
   c. the big elephant was no help.